The Call of the Wild

Jack London

TEACHER GUIDE

NOTE:

The trade book edition of the novel used to prepare this guide is found in the Novel Units catalog and on the Novel Units website. Using other editions may have varied page references.

Please note: We have assigned Interest Levels based on our knowledge of the themes and ideas of the books included in the Novel Units sets, however, please assess the appropriateness of this novel or trade book for the age level and maturity of your students prior to reading with them. You know your students best!

BN 978-1-56137-138-9

To order, contact your local school supply store, or:

Toll-Free Fax: 877.716.7272
Phone: 888.650.4224
3901 Union Blvd., Suite 155
St. Louis, MO 63115

sales@novelunits.com

novelunits.com

Table of Contents

Skills and Strategies

Thinking
Brainstorming, visualizing

Literary Elements
Point of view, story elements,
mood, characterization,
conflict, climax, similes/
metaphors

Listening/Speaking
Role playing, discussion,
interviewing, debate

Vocabulary
Word mapping

Comprehension
Predicting, cause/effect

Writing
Response journals,
freewriting, descriptive,
news writing, letter writing,
research

NOVEL UNITS: RATIONALE

How do you ensure that the needs of individual students are met in a heterogeneous classroom? How do you challenge students of all abilities without losing some to confusion and others to boredom?

With the push toward "untracking" our schools, there are questions that more and more educators need to examine. As any teacher of "gifted" or "remedial" students can attest, even "homogeneous" classrooms contain students with a range of abilities and interests. Here are some of the strategies research suggests:

- cooperative learning
- differentiated assignments
- questioning strategies that tap several levels of thinking
- flexible grouping within the class
- cross-curriculum integration
- process writing
- portfolio evaluation

Novel Units® Teacher's Guides and *Student Packets* are designed with these seven facets in mind. Discussion questions, projects, and activities are framed to span all of the levels of Bloom's Taxonomy. Graphic organizers are provided to enhance critical thinking and comprehension. Tests and quizzes (included in the Student Packets) have been developed at two levels of difficulty (Level 1=lower; Level 2=higher). While most of the activities in the Teacher's Guides and Student Packets could be completed individually, many are ideal vehicles for collaborative effort.

Throughout the guides, there is an emphasis on collaboration: students helping other students to generate ideas, students working together to actualize those ideas, and students sharing their products with other students. Extension activities link literature with other areas of the curriculum—including writing, art, music, science, history, geography, and current events—and provide a basis for portfolio evaluation.

Finally, teachers are encouraged to adapt the guides to meet the needs of individual classes and students. The open-ended nature of many of the activities makes them useful for most any level.

You know your students best; we are offering you some tools for working with them. On the following page are some of the "nuts and bolts" for using these "tools": a glossary of some of the terms used above that will facilitate your use of the guides.

Bloom's Taxonomy...

is a classification system for various levels of thinking. Questions keyed to these levels may be:

- comprehension questions, which ask one to state the meaning of what is written,
- application questions, which ask one to extend one's understanding to a new situation,
- analysis questions, which ask one to think about relationships between ideas such as cause/effect,
- evaluation questions, which ask one to judge the accuracy of ideas,
- synthesis questions, which ask one to develop a product by integrating the ideas in the text with ideas of one's own.

Graphic Organizers...

are visual representations of how ideas are related to each other. These "pictures"—including Venn diagrams, flow charts, attribute webs, etc.—help students collect information, make interpretations, solve problems, devise plans, and become aware of how they think.

Cooperative Learning...

refers to learning activities in which groups of two or more students collaborate. There is compelling research evidence that integration of social activities into the learning process—such as small group discussion, group editing, group art projects—often leads to richer, more long-lasting learning.

Evaluation Portfolios...

are, literally, portable cases for carrying loose papers and prints. More and more teachers at all levels are utilizing portfolios—product folders—in assessment of student learning.

Process Writing...

is a way of teaching writing in which the emphasis is no longer on the product alone. Rather, students work continuously through the steps of prewriting, drafting, and revision—often through collaborative effort—in order to develop a piece for sharing with a real audience.

SUMMARY

With the discovery of gold in the Yukon came a demand for sled dogs. Capitalizing on this need, Manuel—a gardener on Judge Miller's estate in the sunny Santa Clara Valley—kidnapped one of the judge's dogs and sold him to pay off a gambling debt. When Buck, an intelligent, 140-pound Scotch shepherd-St. Bernard mix, was thrown onto a northbound train, he found that the pampered life he had known was at an end. A man in a red sweater, a professional at dog breaking, thrashed him and taught him a lesson he would never forget: he had no chance against a man with a club.

A Canadian government dispatcher, François, bought Buck, and Buck quickly learned how to work in the traces. He also soon learned how to survive in a an environment where the "law of club and fang" was supreme. He learned to eat quickly so that other dogs wouldn't steal his food; he learned to sleep in an air pocket under the snow for warmth. And after watching a more timid dog, Curly, torn to pieces by other dogs, he became a skilled fighter. The contest for power between Spitz, the lead dog, and Buck finally ended in Spitz's death. Buck proved to be a skilled lead dog, and the mail sled arrived at its destination, Skaguay, in record time.

The exhausted dogs were sold to an incompetent trio of gold-seekers—Hal, his sister Mercedes, and her husband Charles. Overburdened and underfed, several of the dogs died before reaching John Thornton's camp that spring. Thornton warned the group that the ice was unsafe, and angrily cut Buck from his traces when Hal tried to beat him and the other half-starved dogs into pulling the sled still farther. Buck and his kind new master watched as Hal and the rest fell through a hole to their deaths a short time later.

Buck loved his new master without bounds—saving him from drowning, pulling a 1,000-pound load to win Thornton a $1,600 bet—but the call of the wild drew him with increasing intensity. When Thornton and his partner used the money to go east in search of a lost gold mine, Buck spent more and more time in the wilderness—meeting with wolves, hunting for meat, wandering. Returning from one such expedition, he was infuriated to discover that Thornton and his partner had been killed by Yeehat Indians. Buck killed several of the natives, then went off to establish himself as leader of the pack of wolves. His hatred for the Yeehats was an enduring one. Legends grew up about a Ghost Dog who stole from Yeehat camps and killed Yeehat hunters and their dogs. Young wolves with Buck's distinctive markings were seen in the forests of the Northland.

ABOUT THE AUTHOR

Born in 1876 in San Francisco to the daughter of a wealthy businessman and a wandering astrologer, Jack London was originally named "John." When he was eight months old, his mother married John London and nicknamed her baby "Jack" to avoid confusion. Jack grew up in a confusing environment; his mother's mental instability coupled with the nationwide economic depression drove the family from house to house in San Francisco. He attended some classes at the University of California, but was self-educated for the most part. Shy and sensitive as a boy, he experienced extremes of mood during adulthood; he believed in an Aryan master race and had a very difficult time holding on to money.

He spent his early years along the San Francisco waterfront, and described these years in his autobiographical novels, *Martin Eden* and *John Barleycorn*. He held a wide variety of jobs, including newsboy, fruit canner, saloon sweeper, lawn mower, fisherman, and laundry worker. He was jailed for vagrancy and later joined the Alaskan gold rush.

He also traveled widely, and served as a sailor for three years. During his short life, he was a prolific writer (essays, poems, over 100 short stories, and eight novels), but his work was of uneven quality. *The Call of the Wild,* his first novel and best-received work, developed the brute-in-man theme prevalent throughout his writing. This theme is that there is a primitive beast within each of us which might appear at any time, especially under stress. It is the central tenet of a literary philosophy called Naturalism. A socialist, he was influenced by the writing of Marx and Nietzsche, and was jailed once for speaking at a socialist meeting.

He married twice and was constantly in debt despite the fact that he was the highest-paid writer in the United States at the time. Suffering from uremia and nephritis, he committed suicide by overdosing on morphine at age 40.

INITIATING ACTIVITIES

Choose one or more of the following activities to prepare and motivate students for the story they are about to read:

1. **Anticipation Guide** (See *Novel Units® Student Packet,* Activity #1): Students discuss their opinions of statements which tap themes from the story. For *The Call of the Wild,* these statements might include:
   — Dogs can be as smart as people.
   — All dogs have a wild side.
   — Dogs can't worry.
   — Dogs can grieve.

2. **Video:** View the film starring Charlton Heston (100 minutes, color, available from Novel Units®).

3. **Log:** Have students keep response logs as they read. In one type of log, the student assumes the persona of one of the characters. Writing on one side of each piece of paper, the student writes in the first person ("I...") about his or her reactions to one episode in that chapter. A partner (or the teacher) responds to these writings on the other side of the paper, as if talking to the character. In another type of log, the dual entry log, students jot down brief summaries and reactions to each section of the novel they have read. (The first entry could be made based on a preview of the novel — a glance at the cover and a flip through the book.)

Summary	Reactions
Ch.1: _____ _____ Ch.2: _____ _____	(These might begin: "I liked the part where...", "This reminds me of the time I...", "Buck reminds me of a dog I once had...", "If I were Hal, I wouldn't...", "I don't understand why Thornton...")

4. **Prediction:** After glancing at the title and cover illustration, students make predictions about the novel. Ask: What does the cover picture tell you about the story's setting? What is the weather like? What can you tell about the dog shown in the foreground? What does "wild" mean to you? What might the "call of the wild" be? Flip through the book, glance at the illustrations, and note the chapter titles. What problems do you think the story will describe? What type of story do you think this is? (adventure? humorous? mystery?)

5. **Verbal Scales:** After students finish a section of the story, have them chart their feelings and judgments about Buck using the following scales or others you construct. Students should discuss their ratings, using evidence from the story.

Like	1—2—3—4—5—6	Dislike
Domesticated	1—2—3—4—5—6	Wild
Happy	1—2—3—4—5—6	Sad
Active	1—2—3—4—5—6	Passive
Honest	1—2—3—4—5—6	Dishonest
Selfless	1—2—3—4—5—6	Selfish
Proud	1—2—3—4—5—6	Apathetic
Gentle	1—2—3—4—5—6	Aggressive

6. **Brainstorming:** Have students generate associations with a theme that is central to the story while a student scribe jots ideas around the central word or statement on a large piece of paper. Help students "cluster" the ideas into categories. A sample framework is shown on the next page.

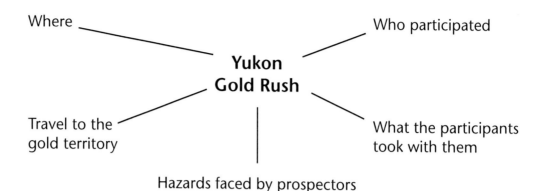

Where _____

Yukon
Gold Rush

Who participated

Travel to the
gold territory

What the participants
took with them

Hazards faced by prospectors

7. **Role Play:** Have small groups of students improvise skits demonstrating one of the following situations (analogous to a situation that is central to the story):
    a) You see someone beating a dog.
    b) You see a group ganging up on a passive classmate.
    c) Someone offers to bet on your dog's strength.
    d) You and a classmate both want to be team captain.

8. **Geography:** Have students examine a map showing North America. Have them find the locations on the route over which Buck is taken: Buck's home in the Santa Clara Valley, California; Queen Charlotte Sound; Dyea Cañon and beach; Dawson; Skaguay (Skagway).

9. **Prereading Discussion:**
    Dogs: Ask how many students have or have had a dog as a pet? How do dogs show affection? What can they learn? How do they act around other dogs? Do they ever do anything that surprises you? How intelligent are dogs? How much thinking, remembering, planning do you suppose they do? How do they establish dominance? How have humans used dogs, throughout history—other than as pets? Do you know anything about sled dogs? What types of dogs are used? Why? How are they trained? What must they do?

    Survival: What special problems are faced by someone trying to survive in a very cold climate? What materials does a person need to survive, for example, in the Arctic? Are the problems faced by an animal—such as a sled dog—different from the problems faced by his master?

    Animal Rights: What rights do you think all dogs should have? Under what conditions should a dog owner punish his dog? How? What rights does a dog have, by law, in this country? What happens if someone denies those rights—for example, if someone underfeeds his dog?

10. **Background Information on the Gold Rush of 1897:**
(Consider having students research the Klondike for homework before discussion.)
- For what is the Klondike known, and where is it located? (famous gold-mining district in the west central part of the Yukon Territory of Canada, bordering Alaska to the west)
- What is the climate there like? (subpolar; average annual temperature is between 25 and 30 degrees F, only above freezing between May and October; January, the coldest month, averages 15 degrees below zero. Temperatures of -50 to -60°F are not uncommon during the winter.)
- When did it become famous? (In 1896 the gold-bearing creek gravels were discovered. A gold rush was underway by 1897, bringing over 30,000 men and a few women.)
- How did most members of the gold rush get to the Yukon? (went to Skagway, Alaska, then trekked over the dangerous White Pass to the Atlin Lakes, then downstream to Whitehorse, Lake Laberge, down the Lewes River to the Klondike)

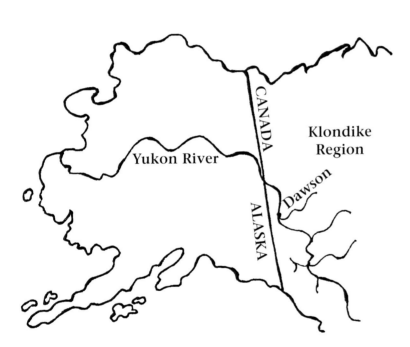

- What was the journey like? (It was long, hard, expensive; many froze to death; supplies were scarce; traders, storeowners, saloon keepers and gambling-house owners often made more money than the miners.)
- Where is the town of Dawson and why was it important during the gold rush of 1897? (It was the terminal for the Yukon riverboat traffic.)

11. **Journal Writing:** Have students freewrite for five minutes, using one of the following sentence starters:
   a) Kill or be killed...
   b) To risk your life for someone...
   c) People behave like animals when...
   d) When there was a gold rush...
   e) Learning society's rules about how to behave...

VOCABULARY, DISCUSSION QUESTIONS
WRITING IDEAS, ACTIVITIES

Chapter 1

Vocabulary

brumal 9	ferine 9	demesne 10	artesian 10
imperiously 10	sated 11	insular 11	progeny 11
unwonted 12	conveyance 13	hydrophoby 13	unkempt 14
assailed 14	waxed 15	gingerly 15	divined 16
surcharged 16	slaver 17	cayuses 18	soliloquized 18
uncowed 19	conciliated 19	weazened 19	dispatches 20
uncouth 20	morose 21	pervaded 22	

Discussion Questions

1. What was life like for Buck, during his first four years? (comfortable and pleasant; He lived at Judge Miller's big house in California, went swimming with the Judge's sons, lay at the Judge's feet by the fire.) How did he stand out from other dogs? ("Ruler" of the domain, he was large, proud, and enjoyed the outdoors.)

2. If Buck had been able to read the newspapers, what trouble would he have known was brewing? (The discovery of gold in the Yukon put large, furry dogs like him in high demand.)

3. "[Manuel] had one besetting weakness—faith in a system" (p. 11). In what sort of system did Manuel have faith? (a system for winning at gambling) Why did this make his "damnation certain"? (He lost money.) How did this faith in a system result in Buck's kidnapping? (He sold Buck for gambling money.)

4. How did Buck get to San Francisco? (He was choked unconscious and thrown on a train.) Why didn't the man responsible for getting Buck there feel that he had been paid enough? (He didn't think $50 was enough for the bites he had gotten from Buck.)

5. As Buck traveled for two days on the express car, how did the express messengers treat him? (They taunted him by laughing, barking, mewing, flapping their arms, gave him no food or water.) Have you ever seen people tease caged animals? Why do you think they do that?

6. In Seattle, the man in the red sweater immediately took Buck out of the crate. What was his purpose? (He was a "dog breaker.") How did he accomplish that purpose? (He clubbed Buck until Buck stopped attacking and let the man pat him on the head.) Do you think he was cruel?

---

7. "[Buck] was beaten (he knew that); but he was not broken." What does that mean? (Buck knew that he couldn't compete with a club, but he wouldn't be cowed; he just wouldn't fight fights that he couldn't win.) What had Buck learned from the man with the club? (Might makes right; a man with a club was a master to be obeyed.) Is that a lesson which some people learn, too? Or does society write different rules for people?

8. According to the narrator, how did Buck feel each time a buyer walked off with another dog? (relieved) Do you think a dog is really capable of fearing for the future? Who finally bought Buck? (Perrault) For how much? ($300) For what purpose? (to help carry the mail for the Canadian government)

9. What was Buck's experience on the *Narwhal* like? (The rolling of the ship sometimes frightened him; there was growing excitement.) What did he learn about François and Perrault? (They were fair-handed with the whip.) What did he learn about the other dogs? (Spitz was tricky, stole his food; Dave wanted to be left alone; Curly was good-natured.) What did he learn about snow? (This cold white stuff that disappeared on his tongue puzzled him.)

10. **Prediction:** Will Buck ever see the Judge again?

Vocabulary Activity

Word mapping is an activity that lends itself to any vocabulary list. A sample framework is provided below. For words that have no antonyms, students can provide a picture or symbol that captures the word's meaning.

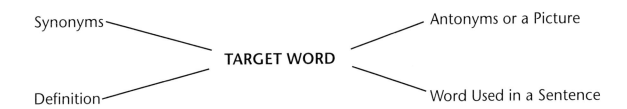

Writing Ideas
a) Write the scene showing what happens when the Judge finds out that Buck is missing.
b) Create the poster the Judge might put up, advertising a reward for information about Buck.

Literary Analysis: Plot

The plot of a novel is the storyline, or order of events. Have students put the following events in the correct order, looking back at the story if necessary.

    ____ a.   Buck was thrown into a train's baggage car.
    ____ b.   Buck was put on a ship stopped in Seattle.
    ____ c.   The man in the red sweater clubbed Buck.
    ____ d.   The *Narwhal* docked and Buck first saw snow.
    ____ e.   Manuel sold Buck to pay off a gambling debt.
    ____ f.   Buck and Curly were joined by two other dogs.
    ____ g.   A stranger choked Buck until he was unconscious.
    ____ h.   Perrault bought Buck for $300.

(Answers: a-3, b-6, c-4, d-8, e-1, f-7, g-2, h-5.)

Geography Activity

On a map of North America, trace the route Buck has taken so far from the Santa Clara Valley to San Francisco to Seattle across Queen Charlotte Sound to the Canadian Yukon.

Chapter 2

Vocabulary

primordial 23	imperative 23	vicarious 23	antagonist 24
assailants 24	draught 25	tuition 25	malignant 25
appeasingly 25	scored 26	diabolically 26	incarnation 26
indiscretion 26	ignominiously 27	disconsolate 27	placatingly 27
arduous 28	trouncing 30	traces 30	fastidiousness 31
malingerer 31	retrogression 32	leeward 33	domesticated 33
cadences 34			

Discussion Questions

1. How did Curly's death affect Buck? (Buck was shocked, had nightmares about it, hated Spitz from then on.) Do you think a dog's dreams could really be troubled by something he had seen earlier? What was the "law of the fang" and how did Buck learn it? (Only the strongest survive; after watching Curly die, Buck fights savagely in future dogfights.)

2. Darwin's theory of evolution was quite controversial at the time this story was written. Where in this chapter do you find an example of "survival of the fittest"? (Curly, too good-natured, died; Buck learned to steal and fight to survive.)

3. How did Buck's life change once he became a member of the sled team?

at Judge Miller's	on the sled team
big house in "sun-kissed" valley	frigid climate
well-fed, ate fastidiously	hungry; stole food; ate fast
swam, hunted, romped with the boys	learned to pull with other dogs— no time for play
king of the place	had to fight to survive
sat by the library fire	discovered how to make a bed in the snow

4. How was François like the man in the red sweater? (Both used force to show dogs "who's boss.") What did Buck learn about pulling a sled? (how to keep the traces clear so that they didn't tangle) Why did he learn so quickly? (He was intelligent; other dogs quickly punished him for mistakes.)

5. Why did Sol-leks attack Buck? (Buck unwittingly approached Sol-leks from his blind side.) Why do you suppose this didn't make the two enemies?

6. What lesson in adaptation to life in the Klondike did Buck learn by watching the other dogs at night? (how to clear a space in the snow and curl up to sleep there)

7. How did Buck's eating habits change from what they were in California? According to London, what was it that "marked the decay or going to pieces of his moral nature"? (He was no longer a fastidious eater; learned to steal food.)

8. In this chapter, what evidence is there that Buck began to remember times that happened before he was born? How is that possible? (Buck had primordial memories of running and hunting with a pack of wild dogs, began to howl like a wolf.)

9. Suppose Jack London had decided to include the information about Buck's former life with the Judge as a flashback. How could he have done this? Do you think a flashback would have been effective?

10. **Prediction:** How will Buck get along with Spitz in the future?

Writing Idea
Curly was attacked by Spitz, but finished off by a pack of dogs. Write an eyewitness report of mob violence among humans. Your report may be fictional, or you may base your report on an actual incident you read about in the paper or heard about on the TV news.

Literary Analysis: Point of View

The point of view is the position from which a novelist tells what happens. The three main points of view are:
  a) *first person*: narration of the story by a character who uses the pronoun "I" in referring to himself
  b) *omniscient*: the narration of a story as though by an all-knowing observer who can see into the minds of all the characters
  c) *omniscient third person*: the narrator is all-observing, but limits himself primarily to what one of the characters can know and experience

Have students discuss the point of view selected by Jack London (omniscient third person; we learn mainly what goes on in Buck's head).

Chapter 3

Vocabulary

precipitate 35	pandemonium 37	marauders 39	dubiously 39
courier 40	compact 41	supremacy 42	preeminently 43
shirked 43	abjectly 44	covert 44	insubordination 44
nocturnal 45	aurora borealis 45	pall 45	travail 45
insidious 46	wan 47	bedlam 47	wraith 48
paradox 48	countered 51	inexorable 52	

Discussion Questions

1. What does London mean by saying that "the dominant primordial beast was strong in Buck"? (Most of Buck's actions sprang from a primitive will to survive.)

2. What was Buck's first encounter with Spitz? (In Ch.1, Spitz had acted friendly, then slyly stole Buck's food.) How did he feel about Spitz in Chapter 3? (Buck hated him bitterly and was jealous of his position as lead dog.)

3. What caused the short, vicious encounter between Buck and Spitz? (Spitz got into Buck's warm nest.) Chart their relationship on the chalkboard using cause-and-effect diagrams. (See following page for an example.)

Cause	**Cause**	**Cause**
Buck has hated Spitz ever since Curly's death.	Buck is jealous of Spitz's position on the team.	Spitz has dared to get into Buck's warm nest.

Effect

Buck and Spitz tangle viciously for a brief moment.

Discussion: What would have happened if the huskies had not shown up just then? (Probably they would have fought to the death if attention hadn't been diverted by the thieving huskies.) Where do you think the huskies came from originally? (Maybe they were sled dogs that escaped, or whose masters died.)

4. Why did the starving huskies invade the camp? (They were looking for food.) Did the sled dogs and huskies fight in the same way? (Starvation made the huskies the more savage fighters.) What fear did the attack raise in Perrault's and François' minds concerning the sled dogs? (They worried that the huskies might have been rabid.) Did this fear turn out to be well-founded? (Dolly later turned mad and attacked Buck, so possibly she had been bitten by a rabid husky.)

5. How did Buck feel as he fought the wild dogs? (The taste of blood excited him.) How did Spitz take advantage of the situation? (Spitz attacked Buck from the side while Buck was fighting the huskies, and later tried to throw Buck off his feet when Buck was about to go after the huskies.)

6. Why did it take the sled team so long to cross the Thirty Mile River? (The ice wasn't strong over the rushing water.)

7. How did Buck undermine Spitz's authority? (Buck kept Spitz from punishing the shirks.) What effect did this have on the team? (They quarreled, worked less hard.) Have you ever seen this same phenomenon affect a group of people?

8. What caused the climactic fight between Spitz and Buck? (Buck led the pack of dogs after a rabbit; when Spitz took a short cut and killed the rabbit, Buck attacked him.) Why did Buck win? (He was the more intelligent, imaginative fighter.) Did the fact that he had once been a "Southland" domesticated dog help—or hurt? (His imagination, nurtured at Judge Miller's, helped.)

9. Do you feel sorry for Spitz? Do you like Buck as much as you did at the beginning of the story?

10. **Prediction:** How will life change for Buck and the other dogs now that their lead dog, Spitz, is gone?

Writing Idea
Read about Darwin's theory of evolution. Explain what he means by "survival of the fittest" and explain how that principle applies to Buck's behavior in this chapter.

Literary Analysis: Mood
Mood is the strongest feeling or emotion in a piece of writing. The terms used to describe the mood of a novel are generally the same words we use to describe a person's mood: angry, sad, fearful, etc. The mood often changes in different parts of a story. Have students reread the passage describing Curly's death (page 24) and examine how the mood in that passage differs from the mood in the passage describing Spitz's death. (The mood of the first passage is one of horror and anger; the mood of the second is one of pride and jubilation—"He deserved it.")

Chapter 4

Vocabulary

obdurate 54	solidarity 56	celerity 56	roundly 56
heredity 59	potent 59	lugubriously 63	floundered 63
convulsive 64			

Discussion Questions

1. How did François react when he found out that Spitz was dead? Why? (He was impressed and relieved; now that the tension was over, the dogs would make better time.)

2. With Spitz dead, who was chosen as lead dog? (Buck) How did Buck make it clear that he wanted that position? (Buck drove Sol-leks out of the lead position, refused to be caught and harnessed in any position except the lead.)

3. Why did the men give in to him? (After an hour, they wanted to get going.) Were they sorry later? (No, he proved to be an excellent lead dog.)

4. How did François and Perrault leave Buck's life? Where? (On arrival in Skaguay, they received orders to go elsewhere.) Do you think he missed them afterward?

5. What did Buck dream of by the campfire on the way to Dawson? (Judge Miller's place, the man in the red sweater, the death of Curly, good things to eat, a primitive man) Why do you suppose he wasn't homesick? (He has reverted in large part to his primitive self and is no longer the dog he was in California.)

6. How was the cook like the primitive man in Buck's primordial memories? Why do you suppose Jack London described them in similar terms? (See diagram on page 17.)

Cook	Dream-Man
"half-breed"	hairy, short
by the fire	by the fire
rounded, muscular	stringy muscles
longer-legged	long-armed

7. Why did the driver put Dave in the harness, knowing that it would kill him? (Dave was miserable when taken out of the harness, refused to run behind the sled, bit through Sol-leks traces, making it clear he still wanted to lead.) Did the driver have sympathy for the dog? (yes)

8. Why do you suppose Jack London refers to the "Scotch half-breed" without giving him a name? What attitude does this suggest? (He is emphasizing the parallel between this man and the anonymous primitive man of Buck's dream.)

9. Why did the "Scotch half-breed" shoot Dave? (He was too sick to pull, and miserable when left behind.) What were his alternatives? How do you think he felt about doing it? Why did he leave Dave in the camp, then walk back to shoot him? (probably so that the other dogs would not witness the killing) How did the other dogs feel? (They knew what had happened and probably realized it could have been them.)

10. How is Buck different in this chapter than he was in the first three? (In the first three chapters, he was learning how to survive in the wild, calling up his instincts; now he is thoroughly acclimated.) How do you think he will behave in the final three chapters?

11. **Prediction:** What will happen to the dogs once they deliver their load of mail to Skaguay?

Writing Idea
Compose one of the letters that Buck and the others were delivering to the gold miners from their families.

Literary Analysis: Setting
The setting of a story is the *time* and *place* of the events. *In what year* does this story take place? (1897; see page 11.) *Where* did Buck live with Judge Miller? (Santa Clara, California) What major U.S. cities did Buck pass through on his way to the Klondike? (San Francisco and Seattle) *In what country* is Buck now? (Canada)

Chapter 5

Vocabulary

feigned 65	recuperation 65	callowness 67	chaffering 67
remonstrance 67	imploringly 69	repugnance 69	suppress 71
superfluous 72	averred 73	formidable 73	cajole 75
copious 77	importuned 78	perambulating 79	innocuously 81
terse 81	irresolutely 82	convulsed 83	

Discussion Questions

1. How far had the dogs traveled in the last five months? (2,500 miles) How were the dogs suffering? (fatigued, drained) Who do you think was to blame?

2. Why didn't the drivers get their deserved rest? (The volume of mail that had to be delivered during the gold rush was immense; the drivers received official orders to go elsewhere.)

3. Why was the team sold? (They were exhausted, had to be replaced by fresh dogs.)

4. What does it mean that Hal and the others bought the team "for a song"? (cheaply)

5. Why had Hal and the rest of his family come to the Klondike, do you suppose? How were they different from other masters Buck has had?

6. How can you tell that Hal and the others were incompetent when it came to planning for a trip through the Klondike? (They packed far too much, didn't know how to secure the load properly.) What do you think of them? What is Jack London's attitude? (He seems to find them foolish.)

7. Why did Hal and Charles buy six extra dogs? (to better carry the heavy load) Why wasn't that a good idea? (More dogs required more food; they hadn't brought enough.)

8. Why did all but five of the dogs die? (starvation) Were the three people concerned about the deaths? (At first Mercedes felt sorry for the dogs, but soon she felt sorry only for herself.)

9. Why didn't Buck get up when it was time to leave Thornton's camp? (He was exhausted and also had a sense of foreboding.) What was Hal's response? (whipped and clubbed Buck) What was Thornton's response? (Thornton sprang upon Hal, told him he would kill him if he struck Buck again, then cut Buck's traces.) How did Buck's behavior save his life? (A few minutes later, the team and people disappeared through a hole in the ice.) (See page 19 for a cause/effect diagram.)

The following graphic, which shows the relationship between ideas in a chain of related events, might help students with comprehension and organization of ideas.

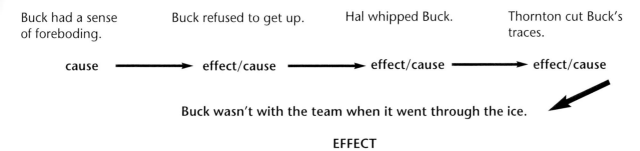

Buck had a sense of foreboding.   Buck refused to get up.   Hal whipped Buck.   Thornton cut Buck's traces.

cause   ⟶   effect/cause   ⟶   effect/cause   ⟶   effect/cause

Buck wasn't with the team when it went through the ice.

EFFECT

10. **Prediction:** What will Buck do "For the Love of a Man" (title of Chapter 6)?

Writing Idea
You are John Thornton. Write a letter to your family in Washington about your new dog and how you acquired him.

Literary Analysis: Characterization
Characterization is the way an author lets the reader know what the characters are like. In direct characterization, the author describes the character directly. In indirect characterization, the author provides clues about the character through thoughts, speech, and actions. What do you know about Mercedes through *direct characterization*? (..."But she was a clannish creature and rushed at once to the defense of her brother" page 69) What impressions do you form through *indirect characterization*? (Her words and actions show her to be silly, selfish, complaining, only superficially concerned with the dogs' welfare; she cries when her excess baggage must be dumped; she insists that the dogs be overfed, then insists on riding when the dogs are weary.)

Chapter 6

Vocabulary
ministrations 86	expediency 86	communion 87	transient 88
mandate 89	peremptorily 89	demonstrative 90	grub-staked 90
crest 90	chasm 91	uncanny 91	tenderfoot 91
provocation 92	mill-race 92	exploit 95	plethoric 97
superfluous 98	virility 98	conjuration 99	

Discussion Questions

1. What was Thornton like? (treated his pets with kindness, outdoorsman, risk-taker, fair-minded) (You might put up this character frame on the board to help students organize what they know about Thornton.)

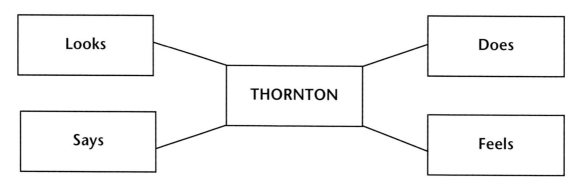

Discussion: Why did Buck love Thornton so much? (He was kind and loving, the perfect master.) Do you think the bond was stronger than with Judge Miller? Why was Thornton such an "ideal master"?

2. How was Buck nursed back to health? (Thornton fed him, let him loaf; Skeet licked the wounds.)

3. How was Buck surprised by Skeet and Nig? (Thornton's dogs didn't seem jealous of him.) Why do you suppose they weren't jealous?

4. Why was Buck uncomfortable when Thornton disappeared from view? (He had already lost several masters.) How can you tell he was distressed? (For a long time, he followed Thornton, never letting him out of his sight.)

5. Do you find it believable that Buck—who had shown such savage behavior a short time before—would act as he did when he began to live with Thornton?

6. Why had Hans and Pete left Thornton behind? (Thornton's feet had frozen the previous December, and his partners had left him to recuperate.) How did Buck treat them when they returned? (only tolerated them)

7. Why did Thornton tell Buck to jump over the chasm? (to show his partners that Buck would do anything he commanded) Do you think he was being childishly foolhardy with Buck's life, or was he surprised himself at Buck's willingness?

8. Why was a meeting called about Buck? (Buck had torn open the throat of a man who had struck Thornton.) What do you think Thornton would have done if it had been decided that Buck must be killed?

9. What did the near-drowning incident, the fight in the saloon, and the sled-pull show about Buck's character? (Buck nearly lost his life to save Thornton from drowning, nearly killed a man to protect Thornton, and pulled a fantastically heavy load to win a bet for Thornton; Buck would do anything for Thornton.)

10. **Prediction:** Will Buck and Thornton ever be separated?

Writing Idea: Newspaper Article
You are a reporter for the *Klondike Kibbitzer.* Describe the remarkable dog-pull you witnessed while chatting with some old-timers at the Eldorado Saloon. Include some quotes from bystanders who know Thornton and Buck.

Literary Analysis: Conflict
Conflict is the struggle between opposing forces which forms the basis of the plot. Have students identify examples in the story of each of the following types of conflict:

Man against Man	(Thornton vs. Hal)
Man against Nature	(gold-seekers and dogs against the frigid Yukon)
Man against Self	(in this case, Buck's internal conflict—behavior learned as a young, domesticated dog vs. impulses to return to life in the wild)

Chapter 7

Vocabulary

whipsawed 104	obliterated 105	flint-lock 105	placer 105
salient 106	tangible 107	commingled 108	hedged 108
pertinacity 109	lope 109	formidable 112	carnivorous 112
compass 112	infinitesimal 112	ptarmigan 113	wantonness 113
palmated 114	simulated 114	ambuscade 114	slake 115
dejected 116	palpitant 116	excrescence 117	usurp 118
incarnate 119	sluice 119		

Discussion Questions
1. What did Thornton decide to do with the money Buck won for him? (look for the lost gold mine) Was that a good decision? What did this show you about him? Have you read any other stories about lost gold mines? How do they usually end?
2. What recurrent dream did Buck have? (dreams about running alongside of the hairy/primordial man) What did the dream symbolize? (Buck's instinctive, primordial memories of his wild origins) Why was Bucking having the dream so often at this point in the story? (He was being pulled by the call of the wild while drawn to Thornton's side.)

3. Why did Buck chase the wolf into blind channels without attacking it? (Buck wanted to make friendly advances, not attack.)

4. How can you tell that Buck felt a conflict about leaving Thornton? (Buck would go off into the woods, then go back to camp and refuse to let Thornton out of his sight.) Do you think he ever would have left for good, had Thornton not been killed?

5. What was Buck looking for when he went off into the woods? (the wolves) How did he survive? (fished for salmon, killed a bear, ptarmigan, chipmunks, rabbits)

6. Why do you think Jack London included the scene where Buck killed the wolverines, who had been eating the remains of the bear he had killed? (to show that like other wild animals of prey, Buck could not only kill for meat, but to defend his kill as well)

7. Why did Buck trap some animals, only to let them go? (He killed to eat, but enjoyed taunting animals such as squirrels, when he was not hungry.)

8. How did Buck select one particular moose from a herd? How did he stalk and kill it? (He had killed a calf, but wanted "more formidable quarry"—page 112. He found a bull that had been hit by an arrow, cut it off from the herd, wore it down by continually bothering the herd, pursuing, attacking, retreating.) Do you feel sorry for the moose? proud of Buck?

9. Why did Buck kill the Yeehats? (He returned to camp to discover that they had killed Thornton, his partners, and the dogs.) How did he feel as he killed them? (He was in a fury during the kill, then proud later that he had killed "the noblest game of all...in the face of the law of club and fang"—page 120.)

10. How did Buck join the wolf pack? How did he become a legend among the Yeehats? (He heard the wolves call, waited for them to come, fought off several attackers; after a half hour, an old wolf sniffed noses with Buck and he ran off with the pack. The Yeehats told stories of a Ghost Dog who stole from camps, slew their dogs, and returned periodically to a certain valley at the head of the wolf pack.)

Writing Idea
Choose a vivid passage from this chapter and recast it as a poem. For example, you might choose the scene describing Buck's raging attack on the Yeehats (pages 118-119). Remove nonessential words and punctuation; experiment with different line breaks. Add a few words of your own, including at least one simile or metaphor.

Literary Analysis: Climax
The climax is the point of highest interest or intensity in the story. It marks a point in the story where the reader is no longer in doubt about the outcome. Where is the climax in *The Call of the Wild*? (Buck returns to find his beloved master murdered.)

22

POST-READING DISCUSSION QUESTIONS AND ACTIVITIES

Post-reading Discussion Questions

1. How does Buck change over the course of the novel? How are people and animals from the "Southland" different from those who are used to the "Northland"?

2. What is the significance of the novel's title? of each chapter title? *(Into the Primitive, The Law of Club and Fang, The Dominant Primordial Beast, Who Has Won to Mastership, The Toil of Trace and Trail, For the Love of a Man, The Sounding of the Call).* The following graphic shows the relationship between a main idea and its supporting ideas (each developed from key details). Students should find it helpful in organizing their ideas about how each chapter contributes to the central idea, or theme, of the novel. Write chapter titles on spokes, details from the chapters on each spoke's flags.

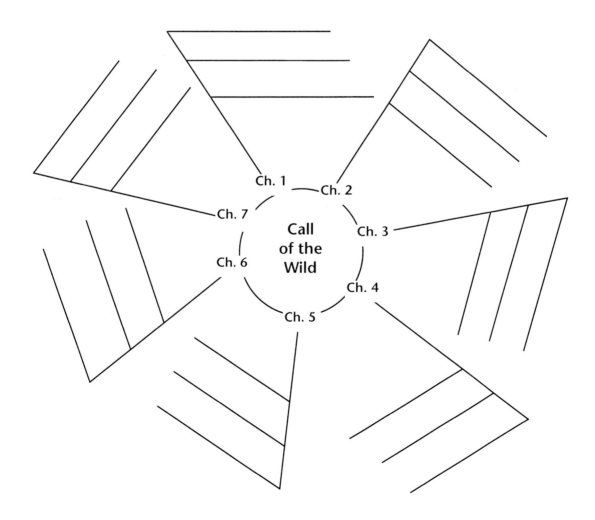

3. As you think back on the novel, what details stick out in your mind? What made the novel so realistic? Do you think London would have been as successful at depicting the Yukon if he had only researched it—instead of actually experiencing it himself?

4. How did Buck feel about each of his masters? How did each affect him? How did he evaluate each of them? How did they evaluate him?

5. What did you think of the ending? How might the story have been different if Thornton had not been killed—or had died a natural death? Why do you suppose London chose to have him violently murdered?

6. What does the poem that starts off the novel have to do with the rest of the story?

7. How much of your own behavior do you think is guided by instinct? How much depends on the family and environment in which you grew up? Have you ever had to change your behavior to adapt to a new environment?

8. Did you find anything about this story to be "romantic"? Does anything about the lives of the human characters appeal to you?

Suggested Further Reading

1. Other novels by Jack London:
    White Fang
    The Sea Wolf

2. Other stories about dogs and wolves:
    Where the Red Fern Grows—Rawls
    The Incredible Journey—Burnford
    Sounder—Armstrong
    Dogsong—Paulsen
    Woodsong—Paulsen
    Big Red—Kjelgaard
    Old Yeller—Gipson
    Shiloh—Naylor
    Julie of the Wolves—George

Writing

1. Write one of the letters that Buck and the other dogs were carrying from family members to adventurers who had gone to pan for gold.

2. Respond to the story with an "alphabet poem." As in an alphabet book, each letter is linked with an image. Here is how you might begin:

   A is the adoration for Thornton
   Buck presents in feigned bites
   Clamping flesh in mock ferocity

3. Write your own short story about a domesticated animal that suddenly finds itself forced to survive in the wild.

4. Write a new ending (three or four paragraphs) that describes what would have happened to Buck if Thornton had not been killed.

5. Write a new ending that describes what Buck's life would have been like if he had somehow been returned to his home in the Santa Clara Valley right after Thornton was killed.

6. Write a scene in which you appear in the novel. Describe how Buck and his owner respond to you.

7. Jack London was very interested in Darwin's theory of natural selection. Write a short essay telling how he develops the idea of "survival of the fittest" in *The Call of the Wild.*

8. Write an essay in which you describe how and why Buck changes over the course of the story.

9. Write a brief essay in which you analyze London's symbolic use of the color red in *The Call of the Wild.*

10. Write an essay in which you describe and evaluate London's use of *anthropomorphism* (attribution of human qualities to animals) throughout the novel.

11. Write an essay in which you support London's Naturalistic philosophy with a contemporary example. Draw a parallel between Buck's return to the wild and a modern-day example of a human being whose "primitive beast" emerged during a period of stress.

12. Write an essay contrasting Buck in *The Call of the Wild* with the central character in *White Fang.*

Listening/Speaking

1. Interview: Stage a mock-interview of several of the people who knew Buck: Judge Miller, Perrault, the man in the red sweater, etc.

2. Debate: Hold a classroom debate on whether Darwin's rule of "survival of the fittest" applies to humans today. (Those who agree get on one side of the room; those who disagree get on the other. Both sides try to convince the undecided group in the middle.)

Drama
1. Rewrite your favorite chapter of the story as a radio play (with a narrator and a few characters). Create some sound effects (e.g., dogs barking, ice breaking, a dogfight) and record your radio play on tape.
2. Act out a scene from the story, such as an argument between Mercedes, Hal, and Charles.
3. Act out a scene that didn't occur—but might have. For example, what would have happened if someone had tried to steal gold from Thornton?

Language Study
1. Make a list of examples of anthropomorphism.
2. Make a list of similes and metaphors used by London.
3. Make a list of naturalistic details included by London.

Art
1. Create an illustrated time line on which you mark central events in Buck's life.
2. Create a shoebox diorama depicting a favorite scene in the story—and including a brief written synopsis of what is shown.
3. Create a new book jacket for the story. (Find photos of Scotch shepherds and St. Bernards to help you figure out what Buck probably looked like.)
4. Illustrate a particularly vivid image from the story, such as the recurring image of the man with the matted hair (page 60).

Music
1. Find some examples of songs that members of the goldrush of 1897 might have sung or listened to.
2. Write a ballad about Buck and set it to music from another ballad (such as "Greensleeves").

Research
Find out more about one of the following topics so that you can evaluate how accurate London's novel is:

1. the behavior of wolves
2. the goldrush of 1897
3. the training and use of sled dogs
4. the geography of the Yukon

ASSESSMENT FOR *THE CALL OF THE WILD*

Assessment is an ongoing process, more than a quiz at the end of the book. Points may be added to show the level of achievement. When an item is completed, the teacher and the student check it.

Name _____ Date _____

Student   **Teacher**

_____   _____   1. Review the story's plot using either a story map, a narrative summary, or illustration.

_____   _____   2. Complete five vocabulary activities.

_____   _____   3. Write a newspaper article to describe the remarkable dog-pull in Chapter 6. (See page 21 of this guide.)

_____   _____   4. Fill in a character web for Thornton. (See page 20 of this guide.)

_____   _____   5. Complete the graphic on page 23 of this guide.

_____   _____   6. Recast a vivid passage from the book as a poem. (See page 22 of this guide.)

_____   _____   7. Choose one of the Writing Ideas from the various chapters.

_____   _____   8. Choose one of the Post-reading Discussion Questions from pages 23 and 24 to complete.

_____   _____   9. Choose one of the Writing Activities on page 25 for a 3-5 paragraph piece.

_____   _____   10. Choose two activities from Listening/Speaking, Drama, Language Study, Art, Music and Research on pages 25 and 26.

Notes